dedicated to our son Francesco
and to all children
who love to color ...

SARA E VITO

HADES
KING OF THE DEAD

HADES
KING OF THE DEAD

APHRODITE
GODDESS OF LOVE

APHRODITE
GODDESS OF LOVE

TO THE PRETTIEST

APOLLO
GOD OF MUSIC

APOLLO

GOD OF MUSIC

ARES
GOD OF WAR

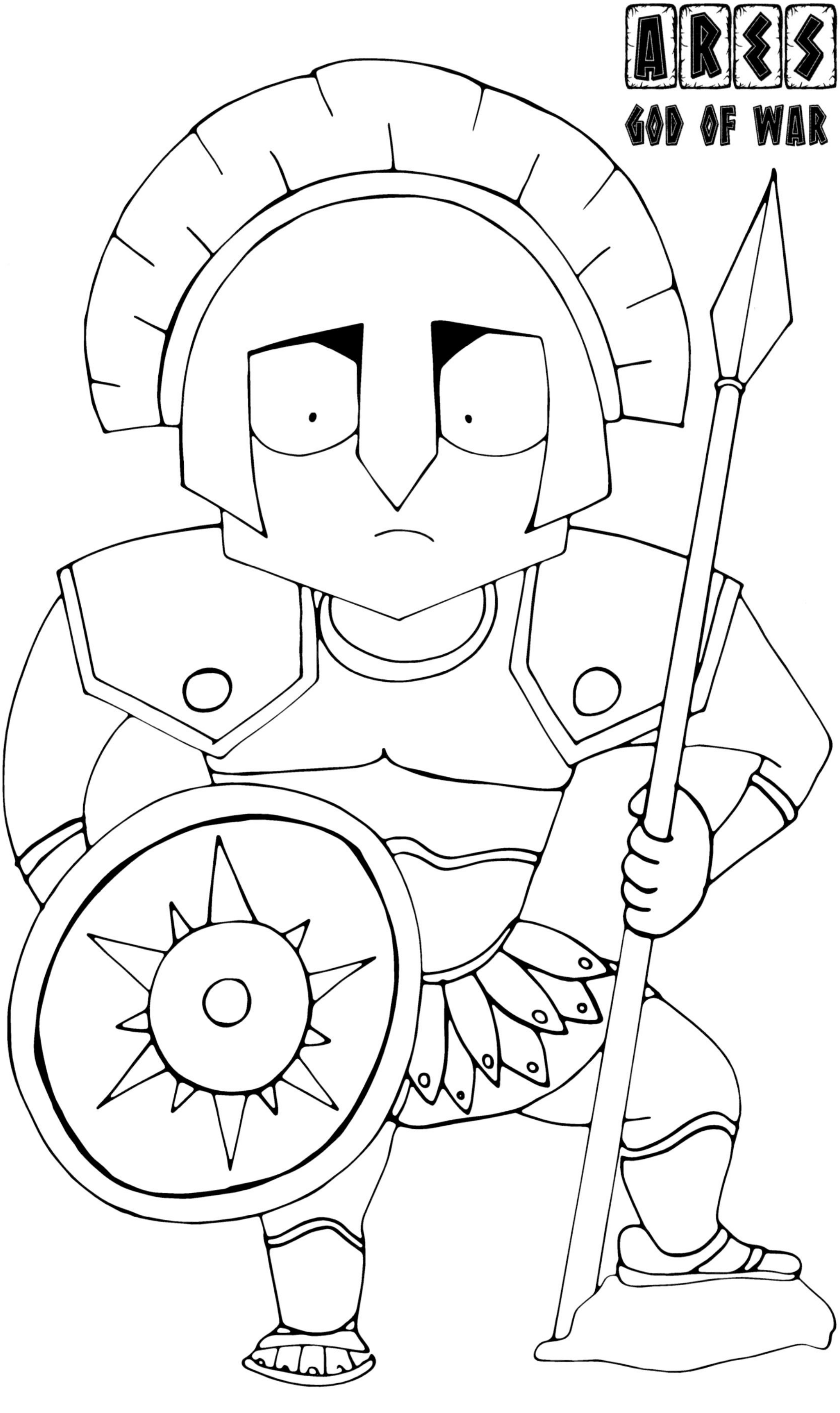
ARES
GOD OF WAR

ARTEMIS
GODDESS OF THE HUNT

ARTEMIS
GODDESS OF THE HUNT

ATHENA

GODDESS OF REASON

ATHENA

GODDESS OF REASON

DEMETER
GODDESS OF GRAIN

DEMETER
GODDESS OF GRAIN

DIONYSUS

GOD OF WINE

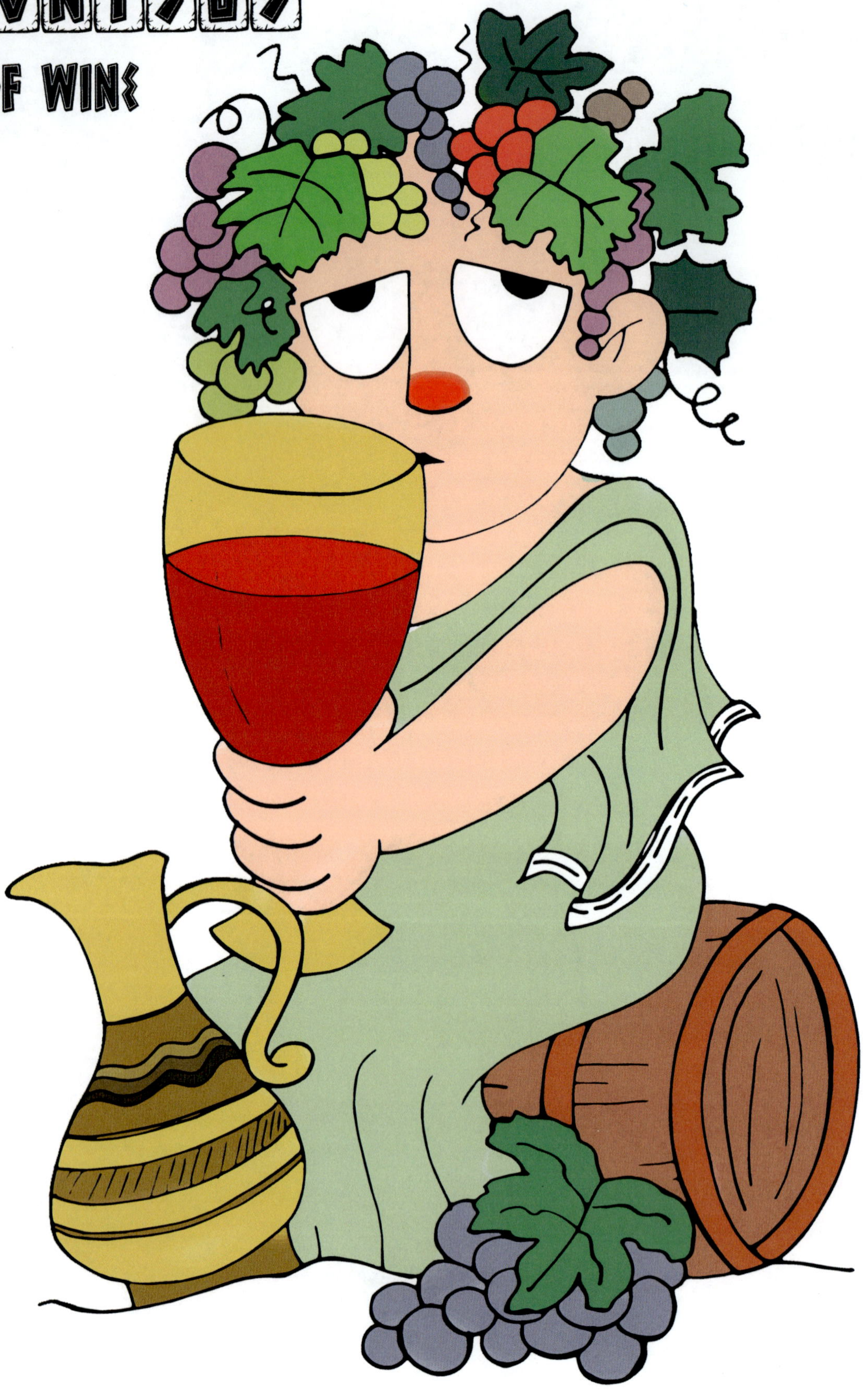

DIONYSUS
GOD OF WINE

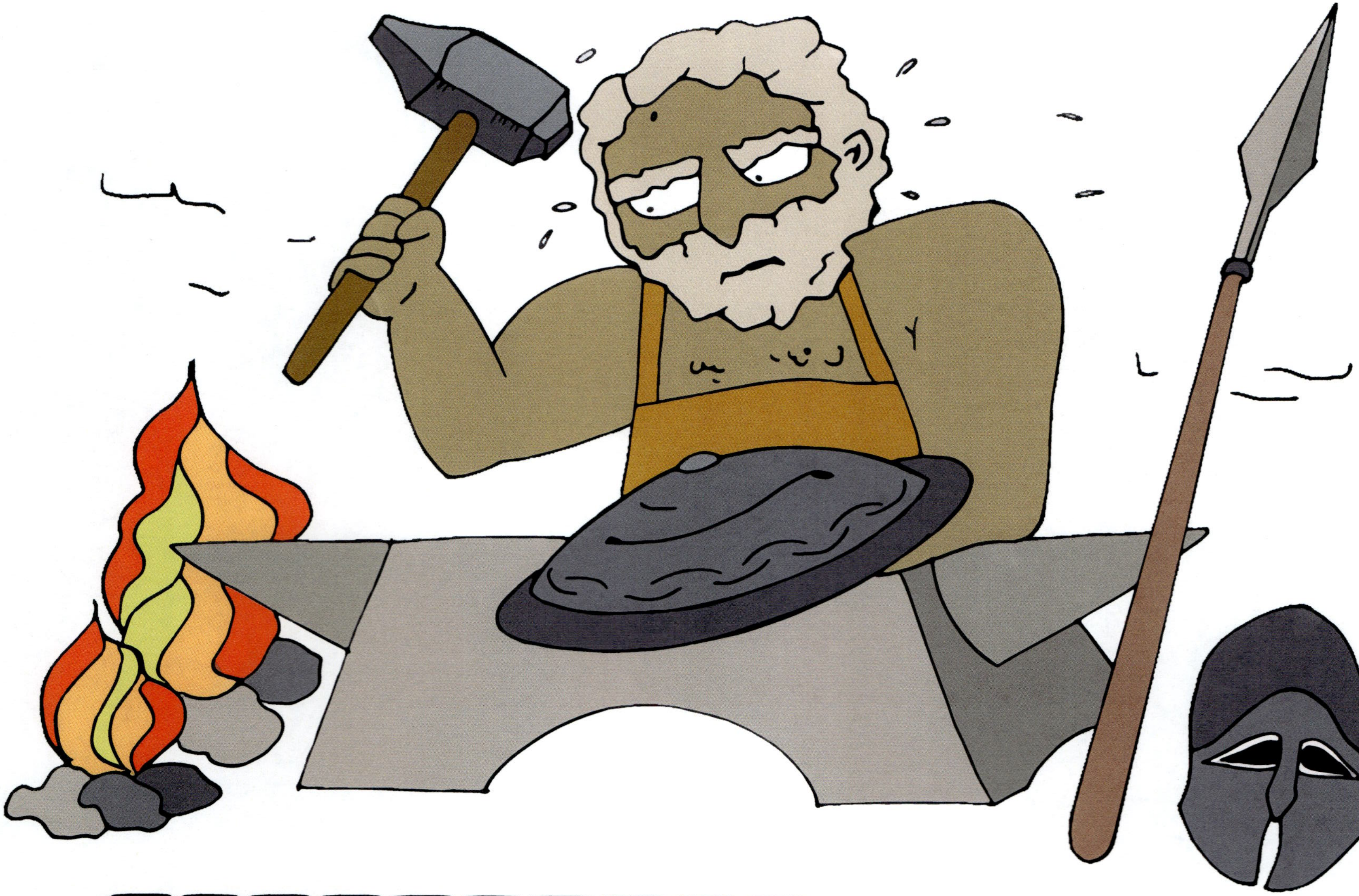

HEPHAESTUS

GOD OF FIRE

HEPHAESTUS
GOD OF FIRE

HERA
QUEEN OF THE GODS

HERA
QUEEN OF THE GODS

HERMES
GOD OF BOUNDARIES

HERMES
GOD OF BOUNDARIES

EROS
THE GOD OF LOVE

EROS
THE GOD OF LOVE

POSEIDON
GOD OF THE SEA

POSEIDON
GOD OF THE SEA

Made in the USA
Monee, IL
11 October 2020